Gifts, Callings and Destiny

©Brian Mgabazi

BRIAN MGABAZI

Copyright ©BRIAN MGABAZI

Gifts, Callings and Destiny

Copyright © 2021 Brian Mgabazi

All rights reserved

Published by Brian Mgabazi Ministries

ISBN: 9798453920730

Dedication

Dedicated to the Holy Spirit and to my Wife Blessing and Our children for whom I love with my life. You are my world, you my love and you, my life. May the Good Lord continue to guide you and that you may walk in greatness, in power and in love.

CONTENTS

Acknowledgments
Thank you to Apostle Samuel Manyika for his trust in me
to use is article that makes the first chapter of this book.
Just through a conversation on Facebook you entrusted me
with the article. God bless you Sir.

INTRODUCTION

The year was 1992 and we were just but three small boys who were at a mission school in Centenary, Zimbabwe. We had such hunger for the move of God. The two Brian's that is Brian Chiyama, Givemore Nyamupfukudza and I, we had developed a close friendship built on the love of God, the word of God and Prayer. Brian Chiyama who was a year older than us had been pushing us to get into a place of prayer and fasting and to seek God more. Every midnight we would meet and pray for at least 2 or 3 hours. Brian Chiyama then in the middle of the school term went home and brought us books by the late Tele- evangelist Kathryn Kulhman and we started reading through these books, as we read them, we started experiencing an amazing power.

 It was as if power moved from these books and landed in our lives. There was such an anointing that when we were reading the books, we began to experience it. We started gathering over 100 students daily in prayer and we began to see the move of God that was amazing. We saw miracles happening, demons coming out and people being healed from the hands of 15-year-old pupils who just had encountered God. St Albert's School being a catholic mission school meant we were not allowed to do any Pentecostal prayers, soon we would have the attention of the authorities of the school. They started hunting for us especially that they could catch us in the act of prayer which was against authorities. Had they caught us this meant immediate expulsion from school. Somehow as small boys we just had faith that God would protect us. We then would gather near the swimming pool on an open field. We were in plain sight but they would look for us and not find us. We would see them passing by and hear them talking to each other, they were told our location but still they could not see us. God somehow covered us in a cloud of his Glory so much that we became invisible to the enemy. Though we were small boys who were just going through their teens, we started a movement that in later years became a non-denominational ministry called Days Men Foundation.

A treasure was found in the deep dirty of a mission school in the middle of nowhere. In later years God blessed Brian Chiyama and he moved to Scotland, I moved to Harare where I started a ministry called Covenant Life Ministries and a number of different organizations among them Apostolic Bishops Network and association of Churches and Church Founders. Givemore Nyamupfukudza became an Apostle and Started the Apostolic Generation Church also in Harare. Having walked such a journey with God I took time to write this book so that I can help someone understand about gifts and callings. The book takes a look at how Gifts are found in the most uncommon places, how you can identify gifts and gifted people. The book helps you to locate gifts and develop them.

Gifts, Callings and Destiny

1.

History of Pentecostalism Growth in Zimbabwe: Apostle Samuel T Manyika

History of Pentecostalism Growth in Zimbabwe: Apostle Samuel T Manyika

The focus on the work of missionaries or those who assisted the Zimbabwean church with resources or any other relevant aid, unfortunately, created the impression that the locals themselves were not involved or did not play any meaningful roles in the evangelization of their country. While it is important to be grateful to all those whom God may have raised to stand with the church in Zimbabwe through any assistance they offered, the fact remains indisputable that local indigenous Zimbabwean ministers were responsible for the meaningful and effective evangelization of this nation.

I say meaningful and effective because there has always been a tendency to evaluate what is happening in the church by focusing on urban ministries, their buildings and the number of affluent people who attend church there. More than 70 % of the Zimbabwean population is found mainly in the rural, small towns, resettlements, farms and mining towns. These were not favorite ministry grounds for most missionaries except those who would be running schools or hospitals.

This big chunk of the population was reached by indigenous churches through their outreach teams. This is something that I have been part of and involved in for over forty years. Occasionally big evangelistic crusades were held by foreign evangelists yielding great harvests of souls. The most effective crusade ministry in Africa in the last 30 or so years, in my opinion, would be Reinhardt Bonnke's CFAN. Bonnke had a sound grip and understanding of how to effectively minister in Africa.

The move of God in Zimbabwe far from having begun in the '70s and 80's charismatic activities actually began in the'20s.While some people may struggle to acknowledge that the Methodist church is probably the biggest influence in all evangelical activity in Zimbabwe that is also an indisputable fact. Many heard the gospel through the outreach programs of the Methodist church. Most anointed apostles of the 30s, 40s and '50s came out of the Methodist church especially those who became key leaders in the Apostolic Faith Church and other independent Pentecostal churches and movements. Even the hymns that most of them continued to use in their churches were and still are from the Methodist hymn book.

At Mukombami in Chikwaka, there was a Methodist Evangelist cum teacher at the only school there, he was called Nicodemus Muzondo. My own grandmother who became the first chairwoman of the Methodist woman's fellowship there in the 30s was actually taught how to read and write by him. He would teach several classes single-handedly and then preach in church on Sundays. He inspired countless young people who became renowned citizens and leaders my father and his elder brother James Manyika being some of them. These were the first people to introduce the gospel and education to diehard African traditionalists. I met Mr. Muzondo in 1969 as a young boy when my father drove the whole of our family to meet him, this was his teacher who also played the role of a spiritual mentor. There was also Mrs. or Mai Chaza, an anointed woman who left the Methodist church because of doctrinal differences after she began to pray for the sick cast out demons and speak in tongues. Thousands came annually wherever this woman was camped to be ministered to. I have first-hand information about her because she was close to my parents.

The apostolic leader Mwazha also taught at the same school as my mother in the early fifties. He was known to cast out devils even at the school assembly. He was a member of the Methodist church but was later expelled, he founded his own church called the African Apostolic Church (AAC). Three brothers who were members of the Methodist church who also got saved and became key members of the move of the spirit in and outside the AFM church were the Gwanzura brothers. These three brothers blazed a trail of miracles, healings, deliverances and accurate prophecies mentoring some of the most prominent members of the AFM church. One of the brothers Enock is the one who baptized the great Apostle Ezekiel Guti, his nickname was vaMachikichori which means feast, this was because when he was preaching it was like the listeners were having a spiritual feast because of the anointing, his eloquence, and knowledge of the bible. John Gwanzura's nickname was vaChihari, meaning clay pot of the Holy Spirit because of the way God used him in deliverance, prophecy and healing. He was also responsible for the salvation of my whole extended family which was tormented by sickness and evil spirits. These men were actually cousins of my father, their grandfathers were brothers who just used different names. The following is an extract from the History of the Apostolic Faith Mission which chronicles how the brothers got saved.

"The Gwanzura brothers played a prominent role in the early days of AFM in Zimbabwe. Tradition says Isaac Chiumbu moved from South Africa to Kadoma with his employer Laurel. Laurel was visiting a relative at Cam and Motor Mine. Both had experienced the baptism of the Holy Spirit with speaking in tongues while in South Africa. In Kadoma, Chiumbu met Paul Karemba and they began to proclaim the gospel. One day as the two were walking, one of Chiumbi's shoes lost a heel. So, they looked for a shoemaker to repair the shoe. They were directed to a shop manned by the Gwanzura brothers, Enoch, John, and Samson. When Chiumbu and his friend arrived, they preached the Gospel to the Gwanzura brothers who believed and were instantly baptized with the Holy Spirit with speaking in tongues.

They left the Methodist church. Enoch Gwanzura proceeded with his ministry to Gobatema, in Gwanda because he could speak English, Shona, and Ndebele, and was helpful to Swanepoel. He moved to various places until eventually, he settled at the Kruger church in Harare. In the meantime, the younger brother John (Johan) Gwanzura, popularly known as Chihari, was active in Masvingo Province. He forcefully spread the Pentecostal gospel in Chivhu (Mupipiti).

By the late 1940's he was stationed at Chatsworth. When he retired, he settled at his farm at Chirau in Zvimba, he continued work at his homestead at the farm after retirement. John (Chihari) Gwanzura had a powerful prophetic and healing ministry. In summer of 1969 when Isaac Mufunguri was bitten by a snake, Gwanzura gave instructions to Isaac's father, Marakia Kuvaoga Mufunguri, who was away from home working with Chihari some twenty kilometers away, that Marakia must go home at once as his son had been bitten by a snake. He was told not to fear as the Lord had intervened and the child was going to vomit the poison. Indeed, Isaac vomited and was well without any medical attention (Isaac Mufunguri). Johan Gwanzura died in 1972.

To adherents of AFM in Zimbabwe, he is the ideal example of what Pentecostalism is all about. He left such a legacy to become a reference point to issues pertaining to Pentecostalism in AFM in Zimbabwe. At his retirement home in Zvimba, he built many mud huts popularly known as 'matumbaevarwere' (huts for the sick). People would come from all over the country and camp there with their food. To many, the food would run out before they recovered in which case, they would receive supplies from Gwanzura's farm."

I never saw Samson Gwanzura but knew Enock and John Gwanzura. In 1964 my grandfather fell sick and was taken to John Gwanzura's farm. John Gwanzura told him that God had added five years to his life. When in December 1969 my grandfather fell ill again John

Gwanzura went to my grandfather's farm in Msengezi near Chegutu and told the family that his time was up. He stayed at the farm for about two weeks until my grandfather passed on. I was thirteen but still, remember everything.

He also stayed at our house in Gweru for a few days sometime in 1970. He loved the hymn Jesu Ndinokuda Muponisiwangu. (I love you Jesus, my savior.) Which he sang with great gusto but off-key. He died in 1972 Enock Gwanzura had an incredible memory, in his eighties, he was half-blind however if he asked you to read the bible, he would tell you to read again if you skipped one word. He practically knew the whole Bible by the head. There are many stories about him. At a certain time, he was called to pray for a sick man, halfway in his journey he was told his own child had fallen sick and he was supposed to go back but he refused and said "the same God on whose assignment I am on will go and heal my child." the child was instantly healed. Another time he was preaching in a church which was next to a football ground the church was almost empty, under the anointing he ran out of the church onto the football pitch, as he ran back to the church people who had been watching football ran after him and filled the church. On another occasion, he wanted to baptize some new converts but the only river nearby was infested with crocodiles. He prayed and the crocodiles were seen crawling to the other side of the river, he got in and baptized everyone.

In 1976 at a ZAOGA Easter Conference at a farm popularly known as kwa Bobo. (Bob's farm) where ZAOGA had been given permission by a white farmer to hold their conferences, I was in attendance and witnessed a miracle after "Sekuru Gwanzura" as he was affectionately called was asked to pray because a heavy storm had gathered and could be seen sweeping towards the tents where the meetings were being held. After he prayed the wall of heavy rain and wind was seen by everyone present turning and heading in another direction.

He actually prayed for me with the laying on of hands two weeks before he died around 1982, I am no longer sure about the exact year. Then there are those who also later came out of the AFM church, teamed up for a while with Nicholas Bhengu the legendary South African preacher but then went their different ways. Most prominent of these is Archbishop Ezekiel Guti whose ministry has touched every corner of Zimbabwe. Apostle Mkwanazi from Bulawayo continued to work with Nicholas Bhengu's Back to God Ministries establishing churches in Zimbabwe. Around the same time, the firebrand preacher Morgan Sengwayo had also come from South Africa and was making waves in Pentecostal circles.

In Ezekiel Guti's ZAOGA were the enigmatic soul winner and preacher Abel Sande a man who practically lived in his tent preaching the gospel planting a church or two every month? Going into places where no one would go. I had the privilege of being in many of the servants of God's meetings and experienced incredible moves of the spirit. These were not your typical city or urban area only preachers. These men would go into places where Satan was worshipped literary. A typical Abel Sande service would see the sick being healed and incredible deliverances from demonic oppression. Despite being a Mukorekore Abel Sande planted churches in every nook and cranny of Zimbabwe. Sounding more like a comedian the man had/has an incredible sense of humor always leaving his audience in stitches before getting down to business. There were other men around Ezekiel Guti though not evangelists they planted churches and mentored many of today's church leaders. There was Raphael Kupara was based in Gweru and spearheaded the growth and establishment of ZAOGA in the midlands and Joseph Choto who was in Bulawayo and saw the establishment of ZAOGA in the Matabeleland region. I do not remember any time I listened to these men and there was not that unmistakable presence of God. These men all had a fear of God that can only be seen in those who have had an encounter with Him.

Around 1979 ZAOGA brought Joe Kayo a one-man spiritual demolition and miracle team from Kenya.

Rarely was such an anointing seen. I was a student in Gaborone Botswana and was with the team of Pastor Mothibi Gaetsiwe and Pastor Tanyala who were responsible for picking him from the airport there and taking him to the train so he could travel to Bulawayo where he held his first meetings with Reverend Joseph Choto of ZAOGA. He later moved to Harare. Believers and non-believers had never seen such a manifestation of power. After he went back to Kenya he was brought back by the late Charles Chiriseri and some University of Zimbabwe Students who came together with the Witness Ministries led by Andrew Wutaunashe. By then the Family of God Churches did not exist. After the University meetings, Joe Kayo teamed up with Andrew Wutaunashe and held countrywide meetings planting churches, this is how the Family of God came to be. Even after Joe Kayo left Andrew Wutaunashe continued planting churches, his meetings were also characterized by outstanding miracles and deliverances, thousands of people got saved. Whatever people think or say about him Andrew Wutaunashe is an authentic and genuine element of the move of God in Zimbabwe. Probably the first preacher to break through to the Zimbabwean intellectual community in a significant way. Most members of FOG were either graduates, college students, bank managers, etc. It is important to know that before this Pentecostalism was highly resented and frowned on and it was mainly the uneducated, peasant's lower class who responded to the gospel. Andrew Wutaunashe appealed to and was given the grace to break that.

In ZAOGA a young preacher called George Chikowa had been raised and was making waves. George and his team were holding large meetings where thousands gave their lives to Christ were healed and delivered. They preached in rural areas, mining towns everywhere. As far as I knew outside of Evangelist Sande's consistent medium-sized but very effective crusades and Reinhardt Bonke's massive powerful crusades which had been seen in Zimbabwe about three times by then, the most powerful crusades of the 80s were the ones fronted by George Chikowa of EGEA, ZAOGA and the Family of God crusades fronted by Andrew Wutaunashe.

On my coming back to Zimbabwe from Botswana in 1980 I was tasked with setting up a College and high school ministry by Archbishop Ezekiel Guti. The ministry was given the name Forward in Faith College and High School Ministries, a name which was used for ZAOGA'S external foreign land-based churches at that time. The team I worked with was composed of myself, the late Miriam Mawaro who later became Mrs Gwese, Pilate Mudavanhu who later founded the His Image Ministries. We were later joined by Musa Gwese who had just graduated from a bible school in Nigeria.

During weekdays we visited all schools which were open to us in Harare, weekends we visited boarding schools. The lives of thousands of students were transformed. Forward in Faith ministries became an established and respected College ministry nationally, holding camp meetings and other events. There are many academics, ministers and others in various leadership positions both in the church, corporate world who got saved through Forward in Faith Outreaches. Many key leaders especially in ZAOGA products of this ministry.

The Scripture Union under the leadership of great bible teachers and leaders like Phineas Dube and others was also doing an incredible job in schools, thousands got saved in scripture union clubs and meetings. Although criticized for its perceived anti-Pentecostal/charismatic stance Scripture Union was not a church and could not espouse a single doctrine, however, they were an effective vehicle of salvation that brought thousands of young people to the Lord.

One cannot talk about the revival that broke out from the late 70s right up to the late 80s especially among young people without mentioning the likes of Richmond Chiundiza, Noah Pashapa, Ngwiza Mkandla, and others. Through Alpha (Abundant life for Christ Ministries) and Faith Ministries which was founded by a former policeman Alistair Geddes who later moved to the states handing over the ministry to Ngwiza Mkandla, many souls especially young people were saved.

I have mentioned the names of those I was acquainted with or those that I knew either personally or through other men of God that I interacted with. Obviously, there are many more in different parts of the country whom God raised during that period to do different things. However, I know that the ones I mentioned here formed the core of these who God used to pave a way for and establish the church in Zimbabwe.

There are many others I did not refer to who have greatly anointed especially two ladies whom God used mightily in my life but who are both late, Mrs. Murape and Mrs. Mugadza who also mentored many leaders and brought thousands to Christ. My late Uncle Meshack Manyika, my father's eldest brother, a well-known Evangelist in AFM and his wife traveled and ministered with John Gwanzura up to the time of his death and were a great source of first-hand information.

It is important to give credit and honor where it is due. I have heard some ministers being referred to as the fathers of the church in Zimbabwe, in my opinion, they are more of spiritual grandchildren.

Sadly, some of these servants of God may have made mistakes or fallen into false doctrine, however, their years of dedicated service produced positive results in the lives of many. People still need to make personal responsible decisions and choices after receiving Jesus.

11.

Eyes that See

Eyes that See

As a small boy around seven years, I was standing on top of a big laundry dish, and I was playing preacher as I imitated the great late evangelist, Arch-Bishop and founder of Ambassador for Christ Ministries Apostle Abel Sande. Apostle Sande in his hay days would stand on the pulpit and shout Zimbabwe is my pulpit as he jumped down. I had seen him do that so many times that as a small boy I began to imitate him.

My Aunt who was there and watching me would laugh and say preach Pastor. Then suddenly my eyes were opened and I saw Jesus Christ coming down from heaven. I was looking straight at the sun and was shouting to my Aunt asking her to look at Jesus. She was shouting back and saying don't look straight into the sun. But as I continued looking Jesus Christ came down and he came to where I was and he started speaking to me. In a conversation that lasted over 15 minutes we spoke. I have no recollection of most things he said except that he wanted me to do his work. He later left me and my Aunt was so perplexed. That was the first encounter that I had with Jesus Christ that changed my life. After that my eyes were so open that I began to understand my calling and what I was carrying. Nobody remains the same after having a heavenly encounter. Learning to hear God is a journey that takes time. In the journey I then had a series of dreams that changed my life completely.

One of the vivid dreams that I had, I was standing beside a river, wearing a fur coat. The place was very cold. Behind me, was a building? I asked people around to tell me where we were as I seemed not to recognize the place. A man said, "We are in Estonia." I then asked what was written on the building and he said to me: "It says Brian Mgabazi Proprietor".

When I woke up, I couldn't understand what the dream meant. I searched on the atlas for Estonia. There was no country named Estonia. The vividness of the dream could not be easily erased from my mind that day. It was just so real. I could not erase the nostalgia around me as I thought of this dream. The problem was I could not understand the dream but I knew it meant something. I wished to understand what it meant. I could not interpret what the dream meant and what was being communicated to me through that dream.

Years later in 1992, the nation of Estonia was established out of the former Union Soviet Socialist Republic (USSR). It was amazing that I had seen the nation about three years earlier on, before its birth. From that moment I began to realize that God speaks through dreams. God has a way of communicating His message to His people through dreams. God does speak and he uses dreams to speak and it's easier to hear God and see into the spirit by reason of dreams. It's easy to see who you are once your eyes are opened.

"And the angel of God spoke unto me in a dream, saying Jacob and I said here I am. And he said Lift up your eyes and see, all rams which leap upon the called are ring streaked, speckled and grizzled, for I have seen all Laban has done to you" **Genesis 31 vs. 12 – 13**

Jacob running away from his brother Esau moves and stays in Laban's house. He stays with his mother's brother for 21 years and he works for him for those years. He is in the same place for over 20 years, nothing changes, but in the 21st year he has a dream that gives him an answer and a solution for him to prosper. The answer and solution to all his problems are already in plain sight but Jacob doesn't see it. It takes God to open his eyes for him to see the answer to his challenge that have always been in his face all along.

The presence of eyes does not mean the availability of sight. It's easy to have eyes and still not see. The same country Zimbabwe that people are running away from into foreign lands, Nigerians and Chinese are running to. They probably are seeing something that everyone else isn't. The same woman that one person will divorce another man will come take and she will be a great wife to him. It's easy to be seeing something that other people are not seeing. The same group of people looking at a situation or circumstance will see things differently because some have an eye within an eye. They have an eye that sees deeper and stronger and see the hidden.

A miracle can happen and people don't even see and they don't acknowledge it's a miracle. People can receive a prophecy and it happens and they don't even give a testimony on what happen. They have eyes but they are not seeing. Then another group of people will acknowledge a miracle that others didn't even see.

"And Elisha prayed and said LORD I pray that you open his eyes that he may see. And the LORD opened the eyes of the young man and he saw and behold the mountain was full of horses and chariots of fire round about ELISHA". 2 Kings 6 vs. 17

Elisha had to pray that God can open the eyes of the young man that was with him. The reason being that he saw something in the spirit and the young man that was with him didn't see it. What you see determines your faith, your action and your future. You can not possess what you cannot see. You can look and you still don't see, as long as the eyes you are using are physical and not spiritual you will look and not see. Most people work from the natural realm as such they miss out on a lot of things that God will be doing.

"It is the Glory of God to conceal a thing; but the honor of kings is to search out a matter". Proverbs 25 vs. 2

The Glory of God is in hiding things, hiding gifted people in the prostitute (Rahab), hiding the answer of a nation in a slave (Joseph), hiding the victory of a nation in a boy (David vs. Goliath), hiding the savior of the world in a carpenter's house. The victory of a group of people in a rejected son of a harlot Jephthah. God hides the deliverance of a whole nation of Israel in a man who has anger issues and cannot speak well he is always stammering Moses. The future leader of Israel and its leader is hiding in a servant boy Joshua. So, it's easy to not see what God has put because it's hidden in plain sight.

"I'll give you concealed treasures and riches hidden in secret places, so that you'll know that it is I, the LORD,

the God of Israel, who calls you by name". Isaiah 45:3 ISV

The word concealed treasures or hidden treasures – is mat-mone in Hebrew, which is secret storehouse; buried money or covered. The treasure is buried in a dark place or a concealed place. In other words, in a covert or secret place. The treasure is in the open but darkness is surrounding it so much that without the ability to bring light and having eyes that see in darkness you won't see.

The above scripture needs to be broken down word for word so we can deduce its meaning. Isaiah the prophet releases a prophetic word that's directed to Cyrus who he mentions and calls his anointed, that is Gods anointed. The word anointed one means messiah, or a messianic prince and it was a title reserved for kings, priests or saints as the consecrated ones of God. Cyrus is a King of Persia and conqueror of Babylon; first ruler of Persia to make a decree allowing the Israelite exiles to return to Jerusalem.

They are a few facts that are established that though he is a gentile he is the anointed one of God, and Gods hand is on him. God is using his hand to subdue nations and God is opening every gate before him. God himself will go before Cyrus and make all the crooked places straight. Then God will release the TREASURES of DARKNESS. The word treasure is the Word O-tsar which is the storehouse of all-important things like silver, gold and armor. These are concealed things hidden from the world, hidden from people, hidden from all around. It's not easily noticed and seen, it's totally concealed. These treasures of darkness are also expressed as HIDDEN RICHES of SECRET PLACES. Hidden riches are concealed wealth, covered glory, secret storehouses and its buried treasure and concealed gifts. These treasures are not in the open, they are concealed and hidden from ordinary eyes and you need an eye within an eye to see the secret places that are carrying the treasures. Which means God has many store houses of a lot of things. God has them hidden in plain sight but it requires someone who has the eyes that see deeper than what's revealed. You can pass through a place and then never realize that it carrying treasure because it's concealed from the eye. The ordinary eye can never see the hidden treasures.

So, verse 3 And I will- The will part is to bequeath, it's to purposeful give as by heart intention to someone without a shadow of doubt. The reason that God is giving the treasure is that you may know that Him (Lord) Jehovah – the self-existent One, am God- Elohim- which is plural which denotes his divinity. God is establishing that he alone is God and he alone is the all-powerful and all-knowing self-existent one. He then is releasing the hidden treasures to his anointed one. This scripture leads us to the teaching of Jesus in the book of Mathew.

"Again, the kingdom of heaven is like unto treasure hid in a field that which when a man has found, he hid it, and for joy he went and sold everything he had and bought that field." Mathew 13:44 KJV

The Kingdom of heaven not the Kingdom of God, the Kingdom of heaven is like a treasure. Now the Kingdom of Heaven is the abode of God, it's the reality whilst earth is the shadow of the reality which is heaven. Heaven as the scriptures says has the streets of Gold, it has the perfect life style that's devoid of death and pain, it's the ultimate life it carries the ZOE- life as God has it. So that Kingdom is like a treasure, hid in a field.

All treasures are hidden in a field, there are many fields of life, business, marriage, family, ministry and all other fields of life. In all those fields there are treasures that are hidden. Then there are the dark places or the secret places that also treasures are hidden. Breaking this verse down a bit, the verse establishes one thing that TRESURE is HID- the issue becomes who HID the treasure. Looking into the fivefold ministry it all has a job to do in the field of Ministry.

The Apostles job is to Hid the truth into the life of the believer, the Prophet has to find the treasure that was hid, The Evangelist has to go and find the treasure and the Pastor and teach have to keep the treasure. There are people that can look at now and they look useless but then later on you realize they are a treasure that was hidden in a field. It's easy to look now and immediately cancel some people because they are in prison or they did something bad. Whilst inside they are carrying great treasure.

The Men is walking and he finds the treasure, weather he deliberately finds it or by accident he finds it but somehow, he finds the hidden treasure. How come the owners of the field didn't find the treasure, how come all that passed that way never saw the treasure but this man sees the treasure. It calls to have an eye that can see what's hidden, what's not revealed, what's not in the open.

When he sees the treasure, he hid it again, and for joy not for the treasure he goes and sells everything and he buys the field. How does he have confidence that the owners will sell the field? He has the audacity to lose everything so that he can buy the field. So, there are treasures that you must lose everything for. Unless you lose everything, you can never get the hidden treasure. Some people must lose their ego, lose their money, lose their savings, lose their sleep that they can get the treasure in the field.

The first level of treasure is treasure in the field the second level is treasure in dark places.

"There is a vein for silver and a place where Gold is refined"

The treasure in the field is the treasure that's easily available within the locality. Then treasure in dark places is treasure in the realms of the spirit that must be fought for and found and released.

III.

The art of Judgement

THE ART OF JUDGMENT

Completing Ordinary level Certificate studies at St Albert's in the November 1993 in Centenary I then went home to Mvurwi. We were members of Zaoga FIF and then same year a Friend and Mentor had completed his Advanced Level, Pastor Gerald Veva. In Mvurwi from December to around March of 1994 we went through as season of serious prayer. We would fast daily from Monday to Friday. Then from 12 midday till 16:00 hours we would be in prayer. In the evenings from 21:00 hours till 02:00 hours we would be in prayer.

Our lives took a serious turn and we started developing in the gifts of the spirit. We started seeing a manifestation of deliverances, healings, prophecy, tongues and interpretation and above all the gift of discernment. We were three of us Pastor Gerald Veva, Gerald my late brother and I. Second term of school year 1994 saw me starting my advanced levels studies at St Philips Magwenya School in Guruve. It was as if all along the months of prayer were preparing me for what I was about to encounter.

Getting to the school I quickly joined up with fellow students and we had the Scripture Union. In the Services we held daily at 5am to 6 am and evenings from 5pm to 6pm daily we started seeing the move of God. We started gathering nothing less than 600 students in the services. There was such a revival at this Anglican Mission school that made the Scripture Union group to be so powerful. To such an extent that a new rule was put that whosoever was voted as the Scripture Union President would automatically become the head boy.

The School started experiencing hysteria outbreaks that shook the school. I would be in the middle of a lesson and the headmaster would come to call me out to go pray for a student who would have gone under attack. As this happened it attracted attention of teachers and thank God some even ended up giving their lives to Jesus Christ. The important lesson was learning the art of judgement, what to do when to do and why to do. Life is a decision-based experience that all its outcome is based on a day to day, minute by minute decisions that we take. The ability to look and assess and make a judgement is of paramount importance. You should be able to look and assess and make an informed decision on what you want to do and how to proceed from every situation.

"Judge not, that ye be not judged. Because the way that you judge others will be the way that you will be judged, and you will be evaluated by the standard with which you evaluate others". Mathew 7:1 -2

Judgment then is the ability to evaluate, the ability to appraise- which is a monetary term that speaks of the ability to look and assess and see worthiness of a thing. So, your ability to evaluate the next move, the ability to evaluate what is surrounding you then exposes you to other people's evaluation. Where you are and what you become is predicated on the judgments that you make on a day to day basis.

"I can of mine own self do nothing: as I hear, I judge: and my judgment is just; because I seek not mine own will, but the will of the Father which hath sent me". John 5:30

The key to a good judgment is premised on knowing and understanding the will of God. The will of God is one of the greatest struggles that anyone will go through. The will of God has tendency of clashing with the human will. Any judgment that isn't based on the will of God will come to nothing. Jesus establishes a fact that all that he does is just, it's not fair but it's just. It brings an equilibrium. It's just because he is doing the will of the father.

"But he that is spiritual judge all things, yet he himself is judged of no man". 1Corinthians 2:15

The level of spirituality of any man is the power that he gets to be able to make the right kind of judgment. The majority of loses in the lives of people are in direct proportion to their lack of spirituality and having the spiritual eyes that can see. The more spiritual a man is the more he calculates and make the right kind of decisions. It's important for every man to develop their spiritual life and grow in their spirituality especially through prayer and fasting. The more a man prays and fasts the more he will grow in the things of God and can easily be able to judge all things according to the way God judges them. Our example or blue print of all things is Jesus Christ. We are made in the image of God and such our view of things should be from the view point of God. We should see as God sees; we should look at things from the eyes of God not the fleshly eyes. Any decision that a man makes from the human eyes is usually very wrong. Our view of things must be from the heavenly view point of things.

"For if we would judge ourselves, we should not be judged". 1Corinthians 11:31

Most people do not take time to judge themselves. They don't take time to look, assess and evaluate. The inability to evaluate is by itself the disaster that causes things to come to a standstill. We then are judged by the world either by our lack of judgment or by our level of wrong judgment. Judgment – is diakrino that means to separate, to discriminate, to have an opinion, to rule to govern.

Everyone who is a driver must learn the art of how one judges the distance between them and the next car. How you then judge depends on your sight and view of things. Sometimes you have then to wear spectacles so that you adjust your sight because if your sight is blurred and then your judgment is wrong. So many times, people are in accidents simply because they have had a blurred view and wrong judgment. Marital accidents, financial ruin and relationship blunders come simply because of wrong judgments.

We judge all things according to a number of things

1. According to what we see, therefore the question is what you are seeing? What are you seeing in your life, in your future, in yourself and in people that are surrounding you?
2. According to what we hear, therefore what are you hearing and whom are you hearing. Every voice that is speaking to you has an agenda.

3. According to how we evaluate things, therefore by what standard are you evaluating everything around you, is it the standard of the word or the standard of your thoughts.
4. According to your knowledge, what you know is important and it's important to increase knowledge.
5. We judge according to our spirituality.
6. We judge things in accordance to the level or measure of our faith.

Any situation presented to us usually needs us to judge it before we act upon the situation. Sickness, Marriage challenges, opportunities for money and business and generally any situation. Eyes can be there but they are dim and they can't see.

"The lord has not given you a heart to perceive and eyes to see and ears to hear unto this day". Deuteronomy 29 vs. 4

"Now Eli was 98 years old and his eyes were dim that he could not see". 1 Samuel 4 vs. 15

"Son of men you dwell in the midst of a rebellious house which has eyes to see and they see not, have ears to hear and they hear note". Ezekiel 12 vs. 2

"Blessed are the eyes which see the things that you see" Luke 10 vs. 23

The above verses establish that we can have eyes and still be in a place where you didn't see well. Which means there are things that can happen and your eye is not able to judge the event and miss the opportunity. We can see gifted people and still ignore them because we are looking from the wrong eyes and wrong point of view. It's important to pray for our eyes to be opened that we can be able to judge correctly. Bishop Noel Jones always says Jesus is not revealed he is only recognized. If Jesus would walk into the room none of us would be able to see that it's Jesus. He is only revealed not recognized. Which means we must be able to judge people and situations correctly if we are to maximize our potential.

"And their eyes were opened and they knew him and he vanished" Luke 24 vs. 31

I pray that we can have our eyes opened. That you can learn the art of judgment. Learn to judge, when to do things and how to do things. The reason why most gifted people never amount to anything is they fail to judge time and moments. It's easy to miss moments and seasons.

IV.

The call of god

THE CALL OF GOD

The year 1995 I remember it as one of the most significant years of my life. I was finishing my Advanced level studies. We had a group of students that were studying together with me. I remember in an open vision I saw questions that were coming in the exam. I then wrote those questions down on paper in the same order in which I had seen them. I then showed the other students and we started studying for our Divinity class. The exam came and the questions were exactly like how I had seen them in the vision.

I was celebrated and became like a demi-god. I was fasting as usual Monday to Friday and I remember God using me to perform so many miracles. So much that by the time I finished my Advanced Levels I even planted several assemblies under ZAOGA FIF. I was being used of God to heal the sick, I was casting out devils. I would preach in church every other Sunday. At school I was the man, I was called Pastor by nearly everyone at school. Like every young man I thought I had arrived. I was experiencing a lot and I was a young man that was seeing so much in my days as a youth. Unlike most people I had walked a journey and began to see my calling. The sad thing in life is that most people get to that place that they die without having known their callings and gifts. One man of God said the graveyard is the richest place in the world because so many people took with them their potential and their gifts. So many unwritten books are in the grave, so many unsung songs are in the grave yard. So many potential million-dollar businesses are in the graveyard.

"In the same way, the last will be first, and the first will be last, because many are called, but few are chosen. We will address the first part which is the issue of calling". Mathew 20:16 ISV

"For God's gifts and calling never change". Romans 11:29 ISV

Now there are many people who are called by God, and their callings are all different. We all are called differently and for different purposes. I have met so many people who are moving around aimlessly without a plan or a purpose but at the same time they do have a calling. Now identifying that you are called is the first part. We will therefore look at the issue of calling so we can understand what a calling is and what it entails.

How do I know I am called?
1. Some people are called whilst in their mother's womb people like Jeremiah. The calling is there and will always be visible from the day they are born. They will be prophesies or something significant about their birth. I have met a lot of people who there is no doubt about them being called into ministry or called into doing the work of God. The birth will be significant or difficulty, something amazing will follow that birth.

2. Some are called along the way of Life like Paul. Some people may find themselves manifesting a calling they didn't know existed before. It's all just a result of God calling them all the way. I have seen people who will live an ordinary life and experience nothing supernatural. But along the way they will then suddenly find themselves doing extra ordinary things.

3. A need in a place may cause a manifestation of a calling. Just because people in a place need a talent that one has, we may see a manifestation of a gift. You can get into a place where they need a preacher and there is no one else except you. God will then use you to minister in the place. The donkey then had to prophesy to the prophet because there was nobody to prophesy.

"I knew you before I formed you in the womb; I set you apart for me before you were born; I appointed you to be a prophet to the nations." Jeremiah 1:5 ISV

Some people are called straight from the womb. As they grow up you can see that there is a calling seating on them. They are moving in power, moving in gifting's that are undisputable. It's easy to see that there is something that's on them. The second Group will have a God encounter along the way, Saul had an encounter with Jesus and became Paul. Moses had an encounter with the fire his Prophetic Mandate and Leadership was confirmed. We then have men like Aaron who are called to priesthood by reason that their brother is a prophet, he is then later called into the prophetic ministry by reason that Moses needs someone to speak on his behalf. When the work becomes too much for Moses, God causes the spirit of Moses to be put on the 70 Elders who become Prophets by reason of the need of the people.

How do I find out my call?

It's usually revealed by your encounter, and encounters can be in a Dream, it can be in a vision or even can be a face-to-face encounter with an Angel or with Jesus Christ himself. We have many that are called but few that are chosen or have encounters. Most of us have had encounters but we didn't realize it that we did.

What are some of these encounters?

1. You may have seen angels in real life or in dreams
2. You may have seen Men of God in a dream telling you that you are called or you keep seeing only prophets or Apostles.
3. You may also have seen yourself preaching or prophesying in a dream.
4. You may even see yourself perform miracles in a dream.
5. You may hear a voice in a dream that then confirm that you are called.

I cannot emphasize enough the issue of dreams, because Dreams are God's way of speaking.

"Then he told the two of them: "Pay attention to what I have to say! When there is a prophet among you, won't I, the LORD, reveal myself to him in a vision? Won't I speak with him in a dream?" Numbers 12:6 ISV

You see God already established you and called you in a dream. Most times we waiting for lightning and a big great voice to say I called you, but God speaks in small still voice and God speaks a lot in dreams. We mostly miss out what he said and what he speaks because we are not sure it's him.

"Then it will come about at a later time   that I will pour out my Spirit on every person.   Your sons and your daughters will prophesy.   Your elderly people will dream dreams, and your young people will see visions".
Joel 2:28 ISV

The dimensions of dreams are amazing. Have you noticed anything important in the Old Testament God would speak through a dream? Dreams are what we call the Gift of the elders. Gift of the mature. It's the dimensions of Open heaven. Did you ever realize that Solomon when he received the gift of wisdom that conversation with God was in a dream? When God was giving a warning about the drought that was coming it was through a dream. So how was Solomon able to make a decision on wisdom? How was he able to make a decision and receive from God? Dreams are a place of transactions, there are spiritual transactions that happens at night as we sleep. Callings are given and even confirmed in a Dream. Most times we want a prophet to come speak or for some super natural voice to speak.

Now another dimension of Calling, God may not have called you. But out of need your Pastor can call you, impart you and you can function. Challenge comes when you disconnect yourself from the Source then your grace cease.

"Do not neglect the gift that is in you, which was given to you through prophecy when the elders laid their hands on you". 1Timothy 4:14 ISV

"The LORD told Moses, "Listen! I've positioned you as God to Pharaoh, and your brother Aaron will be your prophet". Exodus 7:1 ISV

Aaron was Moses Prophet not Gods Prophet. Moses was Gods Prophet. Moses is called by God to prophesy to the People. Because the first duty of a prophet isn't to prophesy but to pray. Moses Main job is to pray for the people. Intercede for them before God. But Moses has a deficit he does stutter as he speaks. And because of that limitation someone must do the job of Speaking. That is Aaron. Now prophets are basically Interpreters. They are not translators. We basically have to understand that. We were to translate what was written on the wall, Mene Mene Tekel ufarsin for Nebuchadnezzar. We could have got a sentence. But when it was interpreted it was 3 chapters. It's the same with tongues that's why they need interpretation not translation. You can speak the same tongue and they mean different things all the times. Because Interpretation and Translation mean different things. Prophets Interpret, the job of Aaron was not to hear God. Moses job was to hear God.

Aaron's job was to interpret what Moses hears, So You have Aaron who hears and understands Moses and listens to his voice. That's why when Moses goes up the mountain to pray Aaron remains behind and build a calf. Because his success in Ministry and call to Ministry is basically attached to Moses. If you remove Moses from the equation, you eliminate Aaron. Moses is not there Aaron is useless. You have to know Your Calling. Is it from God or is it from the Pastor or Apostle? I know of a Man who used to perform miracles. And then he left Zaoga. The miracles ceased. Man, of God can call you and impart you.

Impartation simply means you are a part of someone's grace. The day that you leave that man you lose grace, anointing and relevance. Because it's that man that has the grace you using. You may not have heard God but you seeing things happening. It's the impartation Yes. Your connection determines your anointing and grace. Every man has three things according to Bishop Tudor Bismark- Grace, Rank and Influence. But basically, as a called person you operate by Grace that God gives you.

As time goes on you achieve rank and the rank will give you influence.

"For the gifts and calling of God are without repentance" Romans 11:29 KJV

"For ye see your calling, brethren, how that not many wise men after the flesh, not many mighty, not many noble, are called". 1Corinthians 1:26 KJV

"Let every man abide in the same calling wherein he was called". 1Corinthians 7:20 KJV

"The eyes of your understanding being enlightened; that ye may know what is the hope of his calling" Ephesians 1:18 KJV

The Word Call is Kaleo which is to call aloud- which means you can be called and still not hear that you are called. Which is the place where many are. God loves to hide things. It's the Glory of God to conceal a matter, but it is the Glory of Kings to search it out. Ability to find concealed things is the power of Kingship. The ability to search a matter gives you the ability to possess the place you called to be in, Samuel hears a loud voice calling him. He heard it but still doesn't answer it and he go to Eli whose voice he is familiar with. The issue was Eli voice was so familiar to Samuel so much that when

Samuel hears God speaking, he thinks it's his father Eli Speaking?

It's simple.

a. If you have no earthly spiritual father that you listen to it becomes difficult for you to hear the voice of the heavenly father.

b. It's in the comfort of an earthly father that you get guidance to hear the voice of the heavenly father.

c. In most cases when angels come to you in a dream to speak an important message, they will use the Face and Voice of the earthly father you accept.

The Call is loud but it's easy to miss it. It's crystal clear but in most times, you need someone who has walked the road before who can guide you to be able to understand that this is the Voice of God. I always say that JESUS is never recognized he is only revealed. The challenge with revelation is that it's hidden it takes a certain ability to be able to know the Hidden things and understand them. If JESUS Would walk in to your church today none of us would know him. That's why on the Road to Emmaus the disciples walked with him but still didn't recognized him. They spoke to him things that he did but still didn't recognize him. It took Revelation. The Issue is you must be able to search out and find your call. The power is in finding the hidden. The Word Kaleo is also to invite. Invite which means there is a place you must be, but you get an invitation to come and join the elect, the separated ones, the called ones. You can be invited to a party and venue given but you still can get lost. You can be invited to an event and still not be able to make it. Challenge is the calling of God is without repentance. God will not change his mind. Most of us are invited. But we are lost because we don't have anyone to guide us. I would emphasize that have a mentor. Have someone who can show you're the ropes and the road to travel.

"There is one body, and one Spirit, even as ye are called in one hope of your calling; 5 One Lord, one faith, one baptism, 6 One God and Father of all, who is above all, and through all, and in you all. 7 But unto every one of us is given grace according to the measure of the gift of Christ. 8 Wherefore he says, when he ascended up on high, he led captivity captive, and gave gifts unto men. 9 (Now that he ascended, what is it but that he also descended first into the lower parts of the earth? 10 He that descended is the same also that ascended up far above all heavens, that he might fill all things.) 11 And he gave some, apostles; and some, prophets; and some, evangelists; and some, pastors and teachers; 12 For the perfecting of the saints, for the work of the ministry, for the edifying of the body of Christ: 13 Till we all come in the unity of the faith, and of the knowledge of the Son of

God, unto a perfect man, unto the measure of the stature of the fullness of Christ" Ephesians 4:4-13 KJV

Let's break this one down, there is One Body - which is the Body of Christ. We may be the eye - Apostle, The Ear - the Prophet - the Nose - the Evangelist- the Mouth the Pastor and The Tongue that's the Teacher. We still are one body. We have different functionalities. We are called in One HOPE- What is that Hope it's the agenda to fulfill the Kingdom agenda. It's the Hope to fully function to build the Body. The hope of your calling. So pretty much we all have callings. Some to preach, some to do counseling, so to sweep the Church some to give Finances for the sake of the Kingdom. Everyone is given grace. Not some but all of us. The measure of the grace is given to each and every one is then according to the gift of Christ. We do not all have grace to preach, we do not all have grace to heal, and we all have grace to do something. What differs then is the gift, some are gifted greater some are gifted less.

Grace versus Gift
You can operate in grace thinking you are operating in gift. You can heal from Grace whilst you think its gift. Most people operate on the grace level and have things happening but never get to actually see it's not gift.

"Wherefore he said, when he ascended up on high, he led captivity captive, and gave gifts unto men".
Ephesians 4:8 KJV

Now when Jesus ascended up high to heaven. He led captivity captive. He gave gifts unto Men. The Ascension of Jesus brought the descending of Gifts. Men were able to receive gifts by reason of his death and resurrection. Which means that you're received. Jesus Christ activated the manifestation of gift that was given in eternity so it can be made manifest in time. Had Jesus not died and resurrected and ascended nothing would have descended.

"And he gave some, apostles; and some, prophets; and some, evangelists; and some, pastors and teachers"
Ephesians 4:11 KJV

Let me mess your Theology a bit, The Scriptures say he gave some Apostles, gave some Prophets, gave some Evangelists, who was given, it was the World so the people In Idutywa Eastern Cape who needed a Prophet he gave them the Prophet, the people in Harare who needed an Evangelist he gave them Paul Saungweme. The people in Borrowdale who needed a Pastor he gave them Pastor Tom Deuschle. He allocated gifts according to need and want of an area. It was the need that he saw that brought the allocation of the gifts and callings.

Every gift is place specific. That's why if you are not called for Midrand and you move to Midrand nothing will come out but if you called for Sunning Hill you and you go there you will prosper. Find your place and find your space. Like I said from the beginning. It's the glory of God to conceal a matter. The power is in the ability to reveal the matter. Every seed is soil specific. If you plan Maize in Binga you will not harvest. If you plant sorghum in Plum tree, you will have a bumper harvest. Are you planted in the right place? The issue is usually you not in the right place.

"The eyes of your understanding being enlightened; that ye may know what is the hope of his calling, and what the riches of the glory of his inheritance in the saints" Ephesians 1:18 KJV

The greatest challenge in life is on our sight. It's on our ability not to see that brings hindrance. Because lack of ability to see what's hidden can make you go through years of labor. You can cut out years of labor by just having eyes that see.

"And the angel of God spoke unto me in a dream, saying, Jacob: And I said, here am I. And he said, Lift up now your eyes, and see, all the rams which leap upon the cattle are ring streaked, speckled, and grizzled: for I have seen all that Laban doeth unto thee.

I am the God of Bethel, where thou anointed the pillar, and where thou vowed a vow unto me: now arise, get thee out from this land, and return unto the land of thy kindred." Genesis 31:11-13 KJV

The Angel of the Lord comes to Jacob and says lift up your eyes and see. The fact that you are looking doesn't mean you are seeing. You can look and stare and still not able to see what's right in front of you. The same woman that every other man may be not looking another man will look and see a wife. The wife was always in the woman, but one man just saw a lady another saw a wife. It depends on the eye that's seeing.

"And Joshua the son of Nun sent out of Shittim two men to spy secretly, saying, go view the land, even Jericho. And they went, and came into a harlot's house, named Rahab, and lodged there." Joshua 2:1 KJV

Rahab was known as the neighborhood prostitute. So, some were seeing a prostitute and God was seeing the future of the Davidic Nation. It depends on what you are seeing. The eyes of your understanding must be illuminated. They must be opened that you may know.

The Key to life is in knowledge, knowledge is power. What do you know about yourself? What do you know about where you going? What do you know about what

God has deposited in you? You must get to a place of knowing what you carry. You see God was so confident in himself that he called you, gave you an assignment, and gave you a Job to do way before you were born. He is an all-knowing God, so he knew some day you will leave the church, you will drink beer, and you will sleep around. But all the same he still in eternity called you and appointed you. He knew your weaknesses and challenges but was still so confident in himself to still call you.

The key is knowing:

1. it's not about you but about God.
2. Knowing that God will accomplish his purpose no matter what.
3. That you have an assignment and its success is predicated on your searching it out and knowing it. Searching out knowledge and seeking out more knowledge is the Key to accomplishing your calling. You can't walk in what you don't know.

Where do you find the Knowledge?
1. As you study the word, you find yourself in the word. You locate what you called to be in the word.
2. You find it in the wisdom of mentors, and you must find a mentor who will help you and shape you till you manifest what you carry.

3. You find it in the comfort of what you do without being paid for it. If you can do something and just love doing it so much that you can do it without anyone paying you for it. Your calling is there.
4. Lastly you find it in things that irritate you that you feel you must correct all the time.

David's calling was for worship. He found the Kingdom whilst worshipping. He found relevance by worship and demons would come out of the King Saul, everything else that he got was a byproduct of finding his calling. Paul's calling was preaching. The books we read that he wrote were just byproducts of his preaching. The key is getting knowledge and you will then be whom you are called to be. And so many other things will come as a result of that. It's Like a footballer who owns a Lamborghini. He isn't a driver but a footballer. We may define him by the car but he is a footballer who drives. But what he is simply is, a soccer player. The secret is finding his footing in Soccer. What's your calling? Find it and you will find everything else. It's easy to be called and not gifted. And it's easy to be called and not manifest the gifting. But yes, once people find you gifted, they will try to kill you. That's why when Moses was born many children were killed. When Jesus Christ was born same thing happened.

"And the child grew, and she brought him unto Pharaoh's daughter, and he became her son. And she called his name Moses: and she said, because I drew him out of the water. 11 And it came to pass in those days, when Moses was grown, that he went out unto his brethren, and looked on their burdens: and he spied an Egyptian smiting a Hebrew, one of his brethren. 12 And he looked this way and that way, and when he saw that there was no man, he slew the Egyptian, and hid him in the sand". Exodus 2:10-12 KJV

It came to pass when Moses was grown, he felt something. Challenge with gift is you can be grown but not mature. When Moses is grown there is something is pushing him to do something about the situation. Your calling always makes you uncomfortable about a situation. It makes you irritated. If you have a calling into deliverance, you become uncomfortable with demons and irritated. But key mystery to every calling is time. Key mystery to every calling is knowing when Moses kills the Egyptian he ends up in trouble. And he runs to Jethro's house. Moses grows up in Pharaoh House and he is there for 40 years. God allows him to learn governmental systems. He learns Worldly Financial Systems. He is under a tyranny, who uses murder and authoritarianism to rule? What's in his mind is you kill to deal with people who are against you. Moses gets to believe that this the way that you deal with people. God has to take Moses to Jethro's a priest and a shepherd. He is taught patience as he is looking after sheep. For 40 years Moses is with Pharaoh and 40 years he is with Jethro so that he can have a balance.

You may be called but timing is of importance for you to be revealed. Moses only began to live in his calling at 80. He is now an old man mature, ripe and balanced then finally gets to do what God says he should do, in most cases we rush. Apostle Ezekiel Guti only got to start Zaoga FIF at 35. He is now 98 and has accomplished soo much. Most people usually don't want to go through the process. Sometimes as David you must submit to Saul. God has rejected Saul but all the same asks David to submit. God has refused to have him as leader but still God wants David under a man he has rejected. It's a process of testing your call. Samuel has to be under Eli whom God had rejected. Calling maybe there but gift may not be at the place of manifestation yet. Some are called in the womb some at 5 years but some at 40 but all must go through the process like Moses. Don't have speed. Don't push to do things before time.

"If ye then, being evil, know how to give good gifts unto your children: how much more shall your heavenly Father give the Holy Spirit to them that ask him" Luke 11:13 KJV

Gifts are categorized into two types of Gifts. There are Doma Gifts and Charisma gifts, the fivefold Ministry is where the Doma Gifts falls into then Gifts of the Holy Spirit are Charisma Gift. The word Charisma comes from the word Charis which means Grace.

"For I long to see you, that I may impart unto you some spiritual gift, to the end ye may be established" Romans 1:11 KJV

So Doma Gifts are not a result of Impartation- but divine implantation. You are born with the gift; you are called by Jesus Christ himself and the gift is implanted inside. But Charisma gift can be a result of Impartation- Which we said is being a part of someone gift. You are connected to a Doma that activates the Charisma to operate you can Prophesy from Charisma as a result of your connection to Doma and then you can begin to think you are Doma I hope we caught that

"And he gave some, apostles; and some, prophets; and some, evangelists; and some, pastors and teachers; For the perfecting of the saints, for the work of the ministry, for the edifying of the body of Christ: Till we all come in

the unity of the faith, and of the knowledge of the Son of God, unto a perfect man, unto the measure of the stature of the fullness of Christ: That we henceforth be no more children, tossed to and from, and carried about with every wind of doctrine, by the sleight of men, and cunning craftiness, whereby they lie in wait to deceive"
Ephesians 4:11-14 KJV

The Duty of the Doma is to perfect the Charisma to perform. it's not the Doma Gift that's supposed to be doing it's meant to activate the Charisma to do so that the work become easy. Let me deal with the Doma Gifts first and finish with the Charismatic Gifts.

"Wherefore he says, when he ascended up on high, he led captivity captive, and gave gifts unto men."
Ephesians 4:8 KJV

So that Word Gift in that verse is Doma, It's the descriptive verse for the 5-fold Ministry gifts. Doma are given according to God's own will and purpose. It's a divine Appointment, it's not a human appointment. It's to commit to someone something that already belongs to them. It's important to understand that we are called in eternity but only revealed in time. We are mandated in eternity and only manifested in time. So Doma gifts are the governmental gifts. They are the overall ruling gifts; they are in charge according to the appointment of God.

Doma gifts are enforcers of the Kingdom agenda
    The Apostles are the Eye
    The Prophets are the Ear
    The Evangelist are the nose
    The Pastor are the Mouth
    The Teacher are the Tongue

"And God hath set some in the church, first apostles, secondarily prophets, thirdly teachers, after that miracle, then gifts of healings, helps, governments, and diversities of tongues. Are all apostles? Are all prophets? Are all teachers? Are all workers of miracles? Have all the gifts of healing? Do all speak with tongues? Do all interpret? But covet earnestly the best gifts: and yet show I unto you a more excellent way. They are set in rank, order and influence" 1Corinthians 12:28-31 KJV

Secondarily – Prophets Vs. 31 covet the Best Gifts
The Bible in the Ten Commandments say do not covet but when it comes to Charisma gifts covet them but with the Doma you can't covet. You either an Apostle or you not. You may have title but you may still not have the Call. For the Apostolic Ministry anyone who claims to have a call it's simple, they should have had an encounter with Jesus Christ. You should have seen Jesus Christ and he must have been revealed to you face to face.

"For in the Book of Psalms it is written, 'Let his estate be desolate, and let no one live on it,' and, 'Let someone else take over his office,' who was one of the men associated with us all the time the Lord Jesus came and went among us, beginning when he was baptized by John until the day he was taken up from us. Therefore, someone like this must become a witness with us to his resurrection." So, they nominated two men—Joseph called Barsabbas, who also was called Justus, and Matthias. Then they prayed, "Lord, you know the hearts of all people. Show us which one of these two men you have chosen to serve in this office of apostle, from which Judas left to go to his own place." So, they drew lots for them, and when the lot fell on Matthias, he was enrolled with the eleven apostles". Act 1:20-26 ISV

When replacing Judas, they have to find someone who had been with them seen Jesus' face to face. No one can claim apostleship except they had an encounter with Jesus face to face.

"I am free, am I not? I am an apostle, am I not? I have seen Jesus our Lord, haven't I? You are the result of my work in the Lord, aren't you" 1Corinthians 9:1 ISV

We see it as well when Paul is authenticating his call into Apostleship. The above scripture then shows us that he saw Jesus Christ that automatically authenticates him as a true Apostle. Paul became the Apostle he was because of encounter; the first true mark of Apostleship is Encounter face to face with Jesus therefore. Now how come that one man who used to persecute becomes the biggest preacher. He simply was a learned guy; some are called to be Apostles and prophets. The only thing that will kill you is capacity. Peter could have been the head but Paul takes over because he has capacity.

"But a Pharisee named Gamaliel, a teacher of the Law who was respected by all the people, stood up in the Council and ordered the men to be taken outside for a little while". Act 5:34 ISV

"I am a Jew, born in Tarsus in Cilicia but raised in this city and educated at the feet of Gamaliel in the strict ways of our ancestral Law. I am as zealous for God as all of you are today". Act 22:3 ISV

Paul is educated at the feet of Gamaliel a respected Scholar, that's what gives him advantage. He then is able to speak better, write better. Greatest challenge to Doma gift is Capacity therefore you must increase your capacity and you will be the great man of a Great God. Now Any Apostle can operate in all 9 Charisma Gifts. Though they are about 12 gifts that the Bible mention beside the 9 Charisma gifts that are known. Tongues, Interpretation, wisdom, knowledge, prophecy, faith, healings, discernment, miracles, Helps, Administration, Gifts of Healings. Doma has the capability to operate in all spheres, unlike Charisma gifts. Charisma - means Grace. That's why one day you prophesy the next you can't. One day you can preach well then next you can't. You are in Charisma zone not Doma. A prophet will prophesy no matter what because "The spirit of a prophet is subject to the Prophet. He can prophesy even without prayer because he is A Doma. He can push his spirit to cause him to prophesy. Unlike Charisma. You sometimes prophesy sometime you don't. You can sometimes do things only when the Grace is there. But with Doma it's the everyday matter. You don't push it. You just do it. Charisma Gifts can flow by Connection or by environment. If you in the environment then you can prophesy or heal the sick. The Doma do it by their spirit. When God is calling the 70 Elders who are to Help Moses, the Bible says He took the Spirit of Moses why didn't he take the Holy Spirit, He took the Spirit of Moses and put it on the 70 and they prophesy like Moses.

Because Doma is not Charisma, most People who prophesy and heal are in charisma not Doma. Doma is full time, you are a Prophet 24-7, and you are an Apostle 24-7. You are that, but charisma is Grace and with Grace. -God can give it and take it. With Grace you can tap into it or you can lose it. It's important to evaluate are you really Doma or Charisma?

V.

Gifts and Callings

GIFTS AND CALLINGS

Gifts are meant to prosper in whichever direction they go. The bible says the Spirit of a prophet is subject to the prophet. Therefore, every gift has the ability to prosper anywhere and anyhow, it therefore depends on the person carrying the gift. But it is only a precious stone in the eyes of him that has it. Now a diamond is just another stone to a person in the bush. It's a giver of value to an actor in Hollywood and it's wealth to a collector. Its value is not in what it can do but in the eyes of the person that has the stone. When you have a gift, its value is not determined by anyone else but you. It can prosper in whichever way you take it.

"A gift is as a precious stone in the eyes of him that hath it: whithersoever it turns, it prospers". Proverbs 17:8 KJV

I used to just go and preach everywhere I am invited and would not care. Until I learnt to be intentional in everything. Just don't prophesy everyone and everywhere. Don't be preaching every place. Hear God and be intentional. The prosperity of your Gift is in you making a decision.

"A man's gift makes room for him, and brings him before great men". Proverbs 18:16 KJV

The only thing that will give you what is your own and the thing that establishes your name is your gift. The greatest failure in life is the inability to know, develop and use your gift. The greatest places in life are only reached by those that know and develop their gifts. Room is given by gift, if you are not finding yourself before great man it's not Gods fault, it is yours. When you learn your gift, develop your gift and when you sharpen your gift then spend time in exercising your gift then doors before great man will open. A good example TB Joshua the Late. The man could not speak fluent English. The man could have easily ignored. But he focused on what he did best and he perfected the art.

He was a deliverance guru, He was prophetic, and He was a healing guru.

Though he couldn't preach well he pulled crowds. He met presidents. He ministered to the world. He perfected the art. Pastor Chris Oyakhilome is a good teacher and also into healing. Two gifts that make him who is he is. Most times we have gifted healing people who are not known, because they are trying to prophesy instead of doing what they do best. We have great Mentors who should focus on mentoring and not do deliverance. But most are busy trying to be everything instead of being the best that they are in that area. We cannot be everything to everyone. We have to be specialists in our area of gifting. Nobody can be everything to everyone. Find your area of gifting and focus on that area.

"And Moses did as the LORD commanded him: and he took Joshua, and set him before Eliezer the priest, and before all the congregation: And he laid his hands upon him, and gave him a charge, as the LORD commanded by the hand of Moses" Numbers **27:22-23** KJV

"And Joshua the son of Nun was full of the spirit of wisdom; for Moses had laid his hands upon him: and the children of Israel hearkened unto him, and did as the LORD commanded Moses". Deuteronomy 34:9 KJV

Moses takes Joshua before Eliezer the priest, and before Israel and he gives him charge. The Bible then says Joshua was full of Wisdom because Moses hands were laid on him. Now Joshua is receiving a Charis Gift not a Doma gift like we been explaining. The Doma are the Five-Fold Ministry gifts - Apostle, Prophet, Evangelist, Teacher and Pastor. The Charis are the nine Gifts of the Spirit that everyone who has received the Holy Spirit has access to. But all the same he takes over Israel and leads Israel through with a Charis gift not a Doma.

"And the LORD came down in a cloud, and spoke unto him, and took of the spirit that was upon him, and gave it unto the seventy elders: and it came to pass, that, when the spirit rested upon them, they prophesied, and did not cease". Numbers 11:25 KJV

There are seventy Prophets but God doesn't pick them to lead the children of Israel. He picks Joshua who is carrying a Charismatic gift. Every specific area needs a specific gift. Every specific assignment has its specific gift. The crossing over into the promised Land didn't require prophecy but it required wisdom therefore created a job opening for Joshua. The journey to the promised land required faith and miracles but across the Jordan what was required was Wisdom.

Wisdom helps you function. Whenever you are in a wilderness you will live and walk by miracles, once you cross over you function by Wisdom. No matter How gifted you are the greatest thing of all is Wisdom. Wisdom ladies and gentlemen is the right application of knowledge. The fact that you know there is HIV is devoid of the fact that you can contract. Wisdom is important in how you do anything. Now there are people that can walk into a room and you feel their presence. The moment they get into a place they command a presence. The reason they do so is they have mastered something that most people have not. Everyone right now you building a world around you. The Family, the Business, the Ministry is a world around you.

Your world is simply a reflection of your wisdom or lack of thereof. The Queen of Sheba traveled all the way from Africa to Israel to see the wisdom of Solomon. Because what people spoke of wasn't the gift of Solomon but the wisdom of Solomon. You may be a low gift person like Joshua but you are high in wisdom. Then you will see that you will excel, that is why the bible says in all thy getting get wisdom. A Man like Baba Guti who isn't so articulate in English. a man like TB Joshua who was not proficient in English have been able to build great churches. It's not high gifting its high wisdom, in all your getting get wisdom as a gifted person. The reason why most gifted people do not go far it's because they lack of wisdom.

How Wisdom comes?
1. Wisdom is a spirit and you can receive the spirit of wisdom.
2. Wisdom can be imparted - by talking to wise People wisdom will come to you.
3. Wisdom can be learned. You can study and acquire wisdom.

Get wisdom and your Gift will flourish better. A gift is an enablement that is given by God to an individual so that they are able you to operate in the supernatural realm. Gifts give an ability to do the extra ordinary. There are people who are more gifted than others, they do what other ordinary people would only ever dream of. God makes sure that gifts are given in eternity and manifested in time,

"Jeremiah 1 vs. 5 "Before I formed you in your mother's womb, I knew you and I ordained you a prophet to the nations"

Jeremiah existence is attributed to God and to his eternal plan. God then is saying Jeremiah is what he is and who he is, not because of the relationship between his father and mother but its God who did arrange his existence before the foundations of the earth. So, the very being of Jeremiah is attributed to God and therefore he is on the earth to fulfill the very purpose and agenda God has created him for.

Breaking down this verse we ascertain that: - Before he was formed in the womb. Jeremiah is called already into the ministry whilst in his mother womb, which establishes that calling doesn't locate people at some point in their existence but it is in them way before conception. God calls and gifts some people way before they are even conceived in the womb. The designation of who is who and what gifts they should have was done in eternity and is only manifesting in time. God in his infinity knowledge, wisdom and will already knew Jeremiah, he knew his ability, he knew his gifts and what he would and could do. Before he was born a number of things were established.

He is sanctified- Sanctification talks about separation, consecration, being blessed, purified and made holy. How does God purify someone who isn't yet born and who has not yet sinned is a strange thing? The bible talks about all of us being created in the image of God but as much as we are in the image of Adam we then have sinned according to the nature of Adam. But we hear that God already sanctified him. There is a purifying process of the gift way before the manifestation of the gift on the earth.

He is ordained a Prophet, even before he is born. So, the office or calling that one will carry is a heavenly office, it's given by God himself. It's not given on the earth; it's not defined on the earth it's given in heaven and only manifested on the earth. He gave some Apostles, some Prophets, Some Evangelists, Some Teachers and Pastors. So, everyone has an appointment, has an office, has a duty that is given in heaven and only manifest in time to fulfill the agenda of God. He is apportioned his Territory of Ministry. He is appointed to be a prophet to the nations, not to one but unto many nations.

"Every good gift and every perfect gift are from above, and cometh down from the Father of lights, with whom is no variableness, neither shadow of turning". James 1:17 KJV

There are good gifts and they are perfect gifts and these come from God the father of lights or the father of revelation. It infers that they are gifts that do not come from God. We distinguish the ones from God and the ones from the devil by their goodness and perfection.

"Thou hast ascended on high, thou hast led captivity captive: thou hast received gifts for men; yea, for the rebellious also, that the LORD God might dwell among them". Psalms 68:18 KJV

David in these prophetic psalms is decreeing the death and resurrection of Christ and his establishment of the church. Jesus led captivity captive and he received Gifts for men. There are therefore no gifts that can be given to men outside Jesus Christ. The manifestation of any gift is attributed to the person and ministry of Jesus Christ. God is then coming to dwell among men, how we see it among men, that he is, is through the manifestation of the gifts of Jesus Christ. The moment we see Apostles, Prophets, Pastors, Evangelists and Teachers we know that he is among us.

"A gift is as a precious stone in the eyes of him that hath it: whithersoever it turns, it prospers." Proverbs 17:8 KJV

Gifts are meant to prosper in whichever direction they go. The Spirit of a prophet is subject to the prophet. Therefore, every gift has the ability to prosper anywhere anyhow.

"A man's gift makes room for him, and brings him before great men". Proverbs 18:16 KJV

The only thing that will give you what is your own and it will help you establish your name is the gift. The greatest failure in life is the inability to know, develop and use your gift. The greatest places in life are only reached by those that know and develop their gifts.

"Whoso boasts himself of a false gift is like clouds and wind without rain". Proverbs 25:14 KJV

Not every gift is a true gift. There are pseudo gifts, there are fake and false gifts. The ability to bring full manifestation is what will determine the true gift.

"Every man also to whom God hath given riches and wealth, and hath given him power to eat thereof, and to take his portion, and to rejoice in his labor; this is the gift of God". Ecclesiastes 5:19 KJV

The gift of God gives you the ability to eat and rejoice and enjoy the labor and the fruit thereof. The blessing of the Lord makes rich and adds no sorrow to it.

"Therefore, if thou bring thy gift to the altar, and there remember that thy brother has against thee" Mathew 5:23 KJV

Every gift must be attached to an altar, and every gift must serve and be sacrificed at an altar. The greatest challenge is when we have gifts that are not surrendered at the altar. The Doma and the Charisma gifts must be totally surrendered at the altar.

Luke 11:13 *KJV If ye then, being evil, know how to give good gifts unto your children: how much more shall your heavenly Father give the Holy Spirit to them that ask him?*

Every recipient of the Holy Spirit is a receiver of the gifts of God. Therefore, there is no gift that God will give to his children that is bad.

John 4:10 KJV Jesus answered and said unto her, if thou knew the gift of God, and who it is that says to thee, give me to drink; thou would have asked of him, and he would have given thee living water.

The knowledge of the gift of God is imperative to your ability to ask and receive from God. It's important to research and know.

Act 2:38 KJV "Then Peter said unto them, Repent, and be baptized every one of you in the name of Jesus Christ for the remission of sins, and ye shall receive the gift of the Holy Ghost".

Act 8:20 KJV "But Peter said unto him, thy money perishes with thee, because thou hast thought that the gift of God may be purchased with money".

 The gift of God cannot be merchandised, it cannot be sold with money but it is a result of favor. God watches the intent of the heart more than anything else. There has been a school of thought that says that you give an offering and then gifts are transferred, the bible disputes it.

Act 11:17 KJV "Forasmuch then as God gave them the like gift as he did unto us, who believed on the Lord Jesus Christ; what was I, that I could withstand God"

Romans 1:11 KJV "for I long to see you, that I may impart unto you some spiritual gift, to the end ye may be established"

Charisma gifts come by grace and secondly, they come by impartation. God can give grace or you can have an impartation by serving someone that has the gift.

1Coriantians 12:1 KJV "Now concerning spiritual gifts, brethren, I would not have you ignorant".

The reason why most people struggle in terms of gifts is because of ignorance. Ignorance is a spirit of darkness. It just closes all things and cause you not to experience the best of life. You can never enjoy the life in Dubai if you don't know Dubai exists. The devil will want you to live in ignorance.

1Timothy 4:14 KJV "Neglect not the gift that is in thee, which was given thee by prophecy, with the laying on of the hands of the presbytery".

Gifts are released as a result of prophetic decrees and laying on of hands. The bible then says do not be hasty in laying on of hands because there is always impartation that happens as hands are laid. Most people are

2Timothy 1:6 KJV "Wherefore I put thee in remembrance that thou stir up the gift of God, which is in thee by the putting on of my hands".

VI.

Talents

TALENTS

The first time I stood on a platform was in 1989, I was in primary school and my Pastor asked me to preach. I remember standing up and preaching and I was repeating a preaching by the late great Evangelist Shambach. I preached a good one hour on a word about the Hebrew Boys, Mischeck, Shadrack and Abednego. After the preaching I recall praying for a couple of people. Among them was one lady that had cancer, and another that was bound for an appendix operation. Years later as I am writing this book both of those ladies are still alive and God healed them completely during that service.

I was called to preach that Sunday because naturally I am a speaker. I love people and I love talking to people. These things I didn't work hard to be I just became. Talent is usually a natural ability that is inside. If we want to see that someone is an Apostle, we look at their natural abilities or their talents. The ability to speak or preach, the ability to pull a crowd and to make them to follow. These natural abilities or inborn talents are a pointer to the gift that one is carrying. These are talents

"For the kingdom of heaven is as a man travelling into a far country, who called his own servants, and delivered unto them his goods. And unto one he gave five talents, to another two, and to another one; to every man according to his several abilities; and straightway took his journey. Then he that had received the five talents went and traded with the same, and made them other five talents. And likewise, he that had received two, he also gained other two. 18 But he that had received one went and dig in the earth, and hid his lord's money". Mathew 25:14-18 KJV

Now the Man who was about to travel gave to one five talents, two talents and to another one talent all who were given it was according to their abilities. Talents reflect Charis or grace that has been given to someone. You don't work for it it's just given to you. We have some people who are more graced than others. We have some people who are simply more talented than others. It's according to their abilities. Now let me deal with issue of ability.

"And thou shalt speak unto all that are skilled, whom I have endowed with talent, that they may make Aaron's garments to consecrate him, that he may minister unto me in the priest's office" Exodus 28:3 KJV

"And he has given both him and Ahisamach's son Oholiab from the tribe of Dan the ability to teach". Exodus 35:34 ISV

There are people who have desire to prophesy and then there are people with ability to prophesy, it's natural to them. There are people who are naturally endowed with certain talents. These talents are in their lives so naturally.

1Chronicles 26:31 ISV *"From the descendants of Hebron, Jerijah was assigned chief of the descendants of Hebron. During the fortieth year of David's administration, a search was made by genealogical record, family by family, to find men of great ability, including those found at Jazer in Gilead".*

There are men with great ability and it's just naturally inside. I always say this find your ability and stick to it. I have seen great Teachers trying to be great Preachers and they get frustrated. Simply because they are not focused on their area of great ability. Everyone just by natural disposition you can see your ability. Quite people make great Prophets. Great poet naturally makes great Prophets. Great story tellers and speakers make great Evangelists. It's just a natural disposition they won't struggle. So, locate your ability to find your talent and you will find your gifting.

Ezra 2:69 ISV *"They contributed to the treasury for this work in accordance with their ability: 61,000 golden drachma, 5,000 units of silver, and 100 priestly robes"*.

They all contributed to the treasury according to their abilities. Some are trying to contribute to the work of God not according to their abilities. When you are trying to build the work not using your ability that's why you are under pressure. Pastor Tom Deuschle is a Pastor and a great Teacher and he is contributing to the body of Christ according to his ability. He isn't trying to Prophesy. It's not his ability. He isn't trying to cast out demons or preach, he is teaching and he has a 5000 people church. The key is in knowing your ability.

"Furthermore, for every person to whom God has given wealth, riches, and the ability to enjoy them, to accept this allotment, and to rejoice in his work—this is a gift from God". Ecclesiastes 5:19 ISV

God gives wealth and riches and ability to enjoy them God gives you the talent to speak and preach and ability to enjoy. If you not enjoying it you not in your assignment

"Because he was found to have an extraordinary spirit, knowledge, and understanding, along with an ability to interpret dreams, explain riddles, and solve difficult problems. His name is Daniel, whom the king renamed Belshazzar. Call for Daniel, and he will reveal the meaning of the writing". Daniel 5:12 ISV

Ability to interpret dreams, explain riddles, solve problems. These are the three things that gave Daniel the edge. Those abilities were inside him and made him to be more talented than others and revealed his prophetic gifting. If you can't find the abilities you can't locate the talent you have. If you can't locate the talent you can't see the gift.

Act 2:4 ISV *"All of them were filled with the Holy Spirit and began to speak in foreign languages as the Spirit gave them that ability".*

Finding your Ability

What can you do naturally without having to put yourself under pressure, what can you do naturally without having to push yourself to the limit? What were you born with that you enjoy doing? Ability can be enhanced. The reason why some have made it in life way better than others it's not graces or ability but discipline. You can't make it in life if you are not disciplined enough to grow your ability. It can be grown and it can be perfected.

James 1:17 ISV *"Every generous act of giving and every perfect gift is from above and comes down from the Father who made the heavenly lights, in whom there is no inconsistency or shifting shadow"*.

But it's not up to God to discover your ability to write books, your ability to preach or prophesy. That is left to you. Every gift is natured or watered by prayer and fasting. We have got to a place we have neglected prayer and fasting. Especially in a season where Grace is taught a lot. We can only increase our ability by a number of things.

1. Prayer and Fasting - because you must be willing to pay the price. In most cases the price is separation from the world and we then must be totally separated and must spend time with the Giver of the Gift. The greatest

challenge like I said it's not that there is no grace no. It's that there is no discipline. You cannot live life your own way and expect your gift to grow. The greatest athletes understand the power of practice and discipline. You can't eat whatever you want to eat when you want to be the best athlete. You eat what is necessary to eat so that you can be the best you want to be. There are things that others are doing that you can't do. Others may be watching TV for six hours a day you can't do that. Others maybe having two boyfriends you can't do the same. Soldiers have to go through vigorous training for them to be whom they are to be its important to understand that discipline is necessary. To whom much is given much is required. The fact that you are gifted requires you to be able to control what has been given to you. Prayer is an important thing to help you increase your ability.

2. Ability is increased by knowledge. Doctors go for refresher courses all the time so that they increase their abilities. Managers do the same, it's only preachers who see it as if it's not necessary. Understand that you increase capacity by learning. Learn, read, study, even the prophetic is practiced. You must learn more about it if you going to be sharp at it.

3. Ability is increased by impartation and implantation. Your abilities reveal your talents, your talents reveal

your gifting. Don't neglect your abilities. Learn all you can about your abilities and perfect them.

Romans 11 vs. *29 "For the gifts and callings of God are without repentance"*

The gifts of God once he plants them in you are yours forever. But all the same the gifts may not prosper as much because of you who is carrying the gift. The prosperity of the gift has nothing much to do with God but you.

Ephesians 4 vs. 11 *"He gave some to be apostles, some prophets, and some evangelists; and some pastors and teachers"*.

Gifts are released on the earth to enforce the kingdom agenda. Gifts are empowered and called to pull rank in the realms of the spirit and bring a manifestation of what was set in the heavens in eternity to manifest in time. Gifts work according to your talents and talents are given according to your ability.

Gifts are revealed by talents, so some had five some were given two and then other one according to their several abilities. The more skilled, one become the more gifted he is. Talents reflect Charisma- the grace or favor that has been endowed on someone.

Mathew 25:15 ISV *"To one man he gave five talents, to another two, and to another one, based on their ability. Then he went on his trip."*

Gifts give birth to talents and talents are given according to ability. Let me take time to explain more. Gifts are revealed by Talents. Some had five some twosome one talent. The more skilled and the more talents one has the more gifted they are. Talents reflect the Charisma- the grace of favor that has been endowed on someone. Talents are a physical manifestation of the spiritual gifts that are engraved and enclosed in the inside of the spirit of a being. Talents are given according to one's ability. Your ability is reflective of your talent and your talent reflect of your gift. The more able you are to do something shows your talent?

Ability Vs. Inability or disability
Exodus 28:3 ISV *"You are to speak to all who are skilled, whom I've endowed with talent, that they should make Aaron's garments for consecrating him to serve me as priest".*

Ability
Exodus 35:34 ISV *"And he has given both him and Ahisamach's son Oholiab from the tribe of Dan the ability to teach".*

Exodus 36:2 ISV "Then Moses summoned Bezalel, Oholiab, and all the skilled people to whom the LORD had given ability, including everyone whose hearts stirred them to come forward to do the work".

Leviticus27:8 ISV "But if he is too poor to be valuated, then cause him to stand before the priest and let the priest set a value on him according to the ability of the one making the vow".

SO, VALUE IS BY ABILITY

Deuteronomy 8:17-18 ISV *"You may say to yourselves, 'I have become wealthy by my own strength and by my own ability. But remember the LORD your God, because he is the one who gives you the ability to produce wealth, in order to confirm his covenant that he promised by an oath to your ancestors, as is the case today".*

GREAT ABILITY

1Chronicles 26:31 ISV *"From the descendants of Hebron, Jerijah was assigned chief of the descendants of Hebron. During the fortieth year of David's administration, a search was made by genealogical record, family by family, to find men of great ability, including those found at Jazer in Gilead".*

There are people that have great ability, it is natural in them. There are men that have great ability that will naturally be able to do something.

Ezra 2:69 ISV *"They contributed to the treasury for this work in accordance with their ability: 61,000 golden drachma, 5,000 units of silver, and 100 priestly robes"*.

Ability is the determinant factor to giving. Some people have a greater ability to give than others.

VII.

Enemies of your calling

ENEMIES OF YOUR CALLING

The young man started rising and we all began to somehow look at him with envy. We were assessing his ministry how could he in 2 years do something we had failed to do in 10 years. His ministry seemed to be growing in leaps and bounds. We saw him do things that looked amazing. He was planting one church after another. His Main Church in Harare had an attendance of over 4000 people.

Then he was headlines, the church had shut down and broken into pieces, he had left the country and moved to South Africa. What had happened was that a lady had showed up at his church and he ended up having an affair with her. The long and short was she claimed to be pregnant from the Man of God and all the evidence of their illicit affair were now in public domain. The rest is history. A promising young man with a promising career and growing ministry had died a natural death. The young man had been hit by a Jezebel spirit. Jezebel is a spirit; she will fight anything that's gifted. She will destroy anything that's prophetic and she will emasculate all that has potential. She attacks the mind and bring in suicidal thoughts. When we find Jezebel in the bible, we discover that she was the daughter of Ethbaal king of Zidonians who worshipped Baal. (1 king 16 vs. 31). She has so much control over Ahab to such an extent that he builds an altar of Baal in Samaria. This started a system of idolatry and demonic worship in Israel.

The **Jezebel system** establishes others religions and forms of worship. God has to send Elijah to deal with the system. 1 Kings 18 vs. 4 Jezebel had killed many of the Lords prophets. The Jezebel system kills the prophetic, it fights against the prophetic as it is meant to establish the future. It literally kills and totally destroys the prophetic. This comes in form of women who will seduce and sleep with Men of God. It comes also in the form of spirits that will raise up in churches and stop prophetic expressions.

Herodias system- Wants you to endorse the wrong thing and want you to support its ways. When you don't do it, it will raise up and fight against you and will cut off your head. John the Baptist stands up and rebukes Herodias for what he had done. They then arrest him and put him in prison. They eventually cut off his head. This is a system that will kill you for saying the truth. It's a worldly system that fights the Church.

Sodomic System – The Word Sodom means scorch, burnt that is volcanic it's near the Dead Sea. The Sodomic system is a system that wastes seed, it puts seed in the wrong place. It wastes and destroys seeds. Seed is the most important thing in any system as it establishes the future. The Sodomic system makes pleasure more important than labor so much that pleasure surpass all other things in the hierarchy of needs. The Sodomic system looks at now and never the future. It's one of the greatest systems of moral failure.

Genesis 13 vs. 10 *And Lot lifted up his eyes and beheld the plain of Jordan was well watered everywhere, before God destroyed Sodom and Gomorrah.*

What was enticing to Lot was the outward appearance of the land but the rottenness of it was deep in the inside.

Genesis 13 vs. 13 *But the men of Sodom were wicked and sinners before the Lord*

Sodomic system is wicked, it's a great sin before the lord. There are norms and normal things that God has set that the Sodomic system goes against.

Genesis 18:20 ISV the LORD also said, *"How great is the disapproval of Sodom and Gomorrah! Their sin is so very serious!*

Gen 18:26 ISV *"The LORD said, "If I find 50 righteous people within Sodom, I'll forgive the whole place for their sake."*

Genesis 19 deals with the angelic visit to Sodom. Verse 4 all men of Sodom and Gomorrah encompass the house of Lot both young and old. The system had gotten hold of the whole city. The seed carriers who are the men had become so wicked. They come to Lot demanding that he gives them the men that came into Sodom. They are, rapists and sodomize any new men that comes in. they have exhausted themselves that any new man that comes they want to have them.

Genesis 18:20 ISV the LORD also said, *"How great is the disapproval of Sodom and Gomorrah! Their sin is so very serious!*

Genesis 19:4-9 ISV 4 *"Before they could lie down, all the men of Sodom and its outskirts, both young and old, surrounded the house. 5 They called out to Lot and asked, "Where are the men who came to visit you tonight? Bring them out to us so we can have sex with them!"*

1Timothy 1:10 ISV *"for those involved in sexual immorality, for homosexuals, for kidnappers, for liars, for false witnesses, and for whatever else goes against the healthy teaching"*

Sin- Fear- Mammon Babylonian System

Babylonian System- This is fourth system that we see in the bible. Babylon basically want to use your gift but will not pay for the usage. Babylon will change your name and will want you to worship other Gods. The founder of Babylon was Nimrod Genesis 11 vs. 9. God confused the languages at Babylon. Nebuchadnezzar then established Babylon as an empire and he attacked Jerusalem and he took princes, wiseman and the nobles 2 Kings 24 vs. 11. This is the time we see Daniel, Shadrack, Mischeck and Abednego being taken to Babylon. In Babylon they work for the king, they labor for the king. They are made Eunuchs meaning they can't produce for the next generation. They basically become nothing but just people working to make sure the system goes on. When the Babylonian system enters a church, it will basically abuse people and never pay them. The Babylonian empire starts with Nimrod. Nimrod is the son of Cush and Cush is the son of Ham and Ham is the son of Noah. Nimrod according to Genesis 10 vs. 8 he began to be a mighty man on the earth. He was a mighty hunter before the Lord. His Kingdom started with Babel as he began to build the tower of babel. God declares that we must replenish the earth and subdue it but Nimrod begins to build a tower and the tower must reach the heavens.

Genesis 11 vs. 4 *"And they said, go to, let us build us a city and a tower, whose top may reach unto heaven; and let us make us a name, lest we be scattered abroad upon the face of the whole earth.*

A number of challenges there. Let us build us, and two, let us make us a name. The Babylonian system is selfish, it focuses on you as the individual. It doesn't give glory to God; it says you can do it without the giver of the life and the giver of the gift. Now Nimrod according to archeological finds was a worshipper of the stars. The Zodiac signs were discovered along the ruins of Babylon. Revelations 18 vs. 1– is a system set up to ignore the system of the Kingdom of God. It causes you to be not in partnership with God. It causes you to ignore God. It prides on strength of godlessness. It wants you to trivialize the power of God.

Babylon then had a magnanimous King who was Nebuchadnezzar and he lays siege on Jerusalem and he picks the best of the people to Babylon. Princes, and all vessels of the house of the Lord are carried to Babylon.

Daniel 2 vs. 48 "Then the King made Daniel a great man, and gave him many great gifts and made him ruler over the whole province".

Nebuchadnezzar makes an image of gold and forces everyone to worship it. God has to pull down the spirit of Nebuchadnezzar when he starts saying isn't this the great Babylon that I built.

Revelations 14 vs. 8 "And there followed another angel saying, Babylon is fallen, that great city, because she made all nations drink the wine of the wrath of her fornication".

Revelations 17 vs. 5 and upon her forehead was a name written, MYSTERY, BABYLON THE GREAT, and THE MOTHER OF HARLOTS AND ABOMINATIONS OF THE EARTH.

Babylon makes you to be embarrassed of God. The Babylonian system fights against Daniel, Shadrack, Meshack and Abednego.

People will do things to be famous it's the Babylonian
system

VIII.

Conclusion

CONCLUSION

The secret of a man-
Psalms 144: 3 *Lord what is man that you care for him? Or the son of man, that you think of him? Man is like a breath. His days are like a shadow that passes away.*

Psalms 8 vs. 4 what is man that you think of him? What is the son of man that you care for him? For you made him a little lower than angels, and crowned him with glory and honor. You made him ruler over the works of your hands. You put all things under his feet.

Job 7 vs. 17 what is man, that you should magnify him, that you should set your mind on him. That you should visit him every morning, and test him every moment

The whole fight between God and the devil is about men and his destiny. The whole fight about men is about is seen in the death and sacrifices of Jesus Christ. He has to die and be crucified on the cross just for men. The whole journey that Jesus has to go through is just about man. There is something powerful about men and the devil will do all he can to fight against men.

Therefore, there are a number of things you must watch for as a Gifted person

1. What is your Gifting - Develop your gifting, we all gifted differently. As long as you don't know your gifting you will struggle. Focus on your gifting develop it and be the guru in your gifting. The Bible says your gift shall make room for you.

2. Keep pushing your gifting till Grace finds you. I do believe that you don't find grace, actually Grace finds you. So, you keep doing the best that you can till Grace finds you.

3. Find gifted people that have been put by God into your life. They will be able to help you put your ministry in order and be able to take you to the next level.

4. Be decisive- most ministries loose relevance because you become undecided about going to the next level.

Everyone has a season; you must learn maximize your season. In Zimbabwe there was a season when it seemed God was only moving in Glad Tidings and everyone was going to Glad Tidings. There was a season it seemed the only church that was there was Family of God. The Key lessons there

1. Every Preacher will have their own season.
2. There is a season when every Church will be the only church that's in town. It's the talk of Town. It's scriptural that it will happen. Time and chance happen to them all.
3. If you don't build
a. People when the next wave and big thing happens, they leave.
b. When you don't build in your season that's it when the next big thing happens you will have nothing.

Looking at ZAOGA they have building everywhere same with AFM, how many buildings can you point at by FOG or PAOZ. Every preacher must learn to take advantage of Favor. Because your season of favor doesn't last forever. You will never remain the most sought after, most wanted preacher. Your church will never remain the most loved most wanted church around. You must take advantage of the season of favor. Joseph says to Pharaoh in the 7 years of Plenty let's gather because 7 years of Hunger are coming. Someone with a better preaching style, better Pastoral Style better Excellency than you will rise. You must take advantage of favor. Seasons shift and change all the time. Now take care of a number of things

1. **Weeds** - as you build your ministry, they will be weeds waiting to choke your ministry. The sower sowed but as the seeds came up so did the weeds. Cut off the weeds deal decisively with things in your personal life that are weeds. I had people who were financing me but at the same time they were weeds. It was painful to uproot them but am better off without them now.

2. **Deal with Vision devourers.** - The biggest person you will struggle with is you. You will struggle with personality, family traits, habit and indecision. The moment you can conquer yourself you can conquer the world.

3. The Bible says that any branch that doesn't produce fruit cut it off. There are people that if you don't cut them off in the infancy of your ministry, they will be a mountain of cursing in your life that will be difficult to uproot. Deal decisively with them

Grow in a number of areas

A. Grow in Gifting- Ask some people to check on you and tell you the truth. Are you growing in your gifting? Are you developing? How you preached last year and this year what's the difference. How you healed the sick and now how has it changed.

b. Grow in Grace- Easiness in ministry and life should be evident. You grow by prayer, word and serving

c. Grow in Faith- Without faith it's impossible to please God. Believe for one speaker and believe for land and believe for a building.

So, in your season;

1. Use every opportunity that comes. Buy, store, put aside establish

2. Build Relationships that will help you in the next level

3. Build strategies and plans that will sustain you when you not in demand and not on top. Joseph Principles was setting up a 20% tax and put it up in silos. And in the days when favor was gone, he was able to live off that him and all his people.

What sustain the world when seasons shifted was that? Joseph saw beyond his current season and be planned for the future. Joseph Lived and implemented a Principle. I believe it wasn't popular with people but he still implemented it.

Tips and hinds

1. Mobilize your church to raise money to build. They can even give half their salaries towards building program. A CHURCH WITH A BUILDING WILL NEVER DIE. So as long as we still moving from building to building our churches can disappear.

2. Take advantage of the Politics and get land to build Schools it's what has sustained Methodists and Catholics. They may not be land to build churches anymore but schools will be present and you can put your church on the school land as well. And affect generations. You build one block abs fees will build the next block and the next

Biggest mistake most Pastors make is putting Business persons as Pastors and Elders because they have money. Take advantage of them being there let them be in charge of building fund, bus fund and other fund raising and they will help you build the church. The moment you allow them to be in the spiritual board you going into a big fight

Order Rank and Protocols

The kingdom of God works on Rank, Order and Protocol. There are established Ranks that cannot be broken. Eli is fired by God, but God still gives Hannah her Miracle through Eli. Eli fired by God still mentors the one of the greatest prophets of all times Samuel. The man may have fallen from grace but he still had his rank. It's easy for you to look at a man like Eli and speak Evil of him because he has fallen from Grace but he will still have his rank. You can't speak evil of dignitaries and get away with it. The kids call Elisha bald head and he cursed them. This Generation has so much lack of honor. It's important to understand that you must honor the protocols of the kingdom.

We are in Generation that fails to honor the graces, gifts and dignitaries that have gone ahead of us. The moment someone falls and he has been ahead of us then we have people that will speak evil of them.

1Chronicles 12:33 KJV "Of Zebulun, such as went forth to battle, expert in war, with all instruments of war, fifty thousand, which could keep rank: they were not of double heart"

1Chronicles 12:38 KJV "All these men of war, that could keep rank, came with a perfect heart to Hebron, to make David king over all Israel: and all the rest also of Israel were of one heart to make David king".

There is need to have the ability to maintain rank, order and protocols in the kingdom otherwise we fail to glean from the other generation.

Mantles

Elijah and Elisha

Elijah has the calling of God over his life and he raises Elisha who became his assistant. Elisha by serving Elijah faithfully ends up carrying double the anointing and the grace on Elijah. Elisha ends up carrying the mantle of Elijah. Mantles are basically the grace and the anointing upon a father that will go down to the next generation. It's easier to walk in the grace of someone that had a covenant or a call of God by simply receiving their mantle.

Moses and Joshua

When Moses dies and God is looking for someone to take over Joshua comes up naturally as the next leader. He is just but a servant boy. Joshua become the next leader of Israel by receiving the mantle that was on Moses.

1Ki 18:46 ISV "After Ahab had left, the hand of the LORD came upon Elijah, and he tucked his mantle into his belt and outran Ahab in a race to the city gate of Jezreel".

1Ki 19:13 ISV "As soon as Elijah heard it, he covered his face in his mantle, went outside, and stood at the entrance to the cave. And there a voice spoke to him and said, "What are you doing here, Elijah?"

There are mantles of men like David, Solomon, Samuel and some Apostolic fathers that are there. They need someone to pick up mantles of those that have gone ahead.

ABOUT THE AUTHOR

Brian Mgabazi serves as the Presiding Bishop of Covenant Life Ministries International which incorporates Covenant Life Churches, Covenant Faith Churches South Africa, Covenant Life Ministries Botswana and Igreja Nova Vida Alianca Mozambique, Covenant Life Bible Institute, Brian Mgabazi Apostolic Network and Heal Africa Trust. He is also the founding President of Apostolic Bishops Network which is an association of Apostles and Bishops. He has been in Ministry since 1999 and has been preaching since 1989. He is a renowned conference speaker especially on leadership, Kingdom Order, Kingdom structures and Kingdom Strategies.